Modeling Clay

FAVORITE ANIMALS

bonus
How to draw them

Panda bear

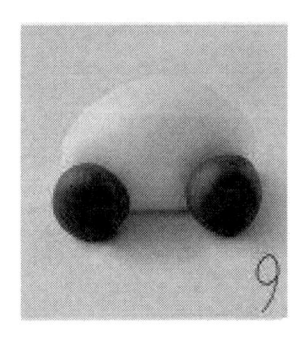

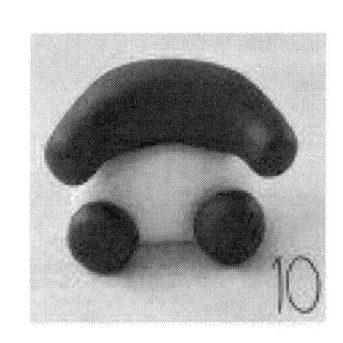

- The panda bear is a large mammal, at maturity it reaches a height of 1.5-1.8 meters and a weight of 190 kilograms. Having no predators, apart from humans, the panda bear can live for 25 years or even more.
- The panda bear has a massive head, heavy body, short tail, round ears, having a gait similar to that of humans.
- The fur of the panda bear is white, with round black spots on the ears, eyes, chest, legs, and shoulders.
- The panda bear lives in China, more precisely in coniferous forests, being a humid and cold environment, suitable for growing bamboo.
- It is a lazy animal with two main daily occupations: sleeping and eating. Panda bears exclusively consume leaves and bamboo shoots. They climb trees quickly and are also good swimmers. They do not make dens, like other bears, because they do not hibernate.
- Panda bears are endangered animals, currently, there are approximately 1600 specimens.

1 2 3 4 5 6 7 8

Draw here

Rabbit

- **What I look like:** I am a herbivorous, rodent mammal and you can recognize me by my long ears and short, bushy tail, by my soft and fluffy fur that varies according to place and season, the general shade being reddish-grey, but it can also be white or black. My ears can be 10 cm long. I have 28 teeth, of which the incisors are constantly growing, so I always have to gnaw on something to keep them at a normal length.

- **How much do I weigh:** my weight is 4 kg, and in some cases, it can reach up to 6 kg.

- **How long they live:** they reach maturity at 6 months and can live up to 10 years.

- **What I eat:** green plants, vegetables: lettuce, cabbage, spinach, lobola, stevia, green beans, peas, bell peppers, cucumbers, and of course carrots.

1. 2. 3. 4.

5. 6. 7.

8. 9.

Draw here

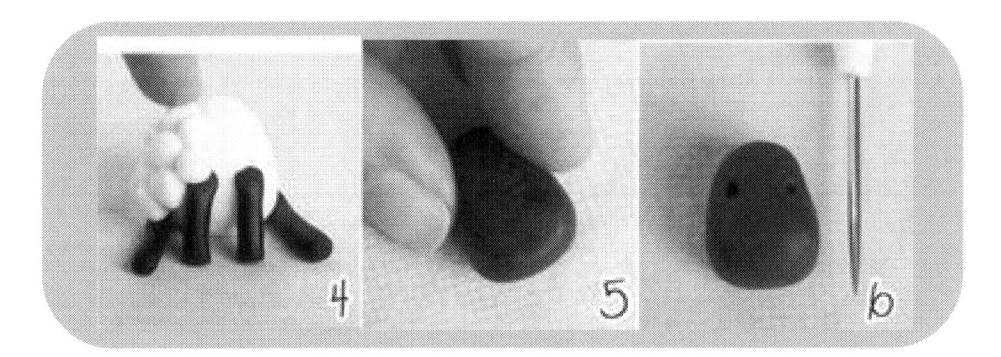

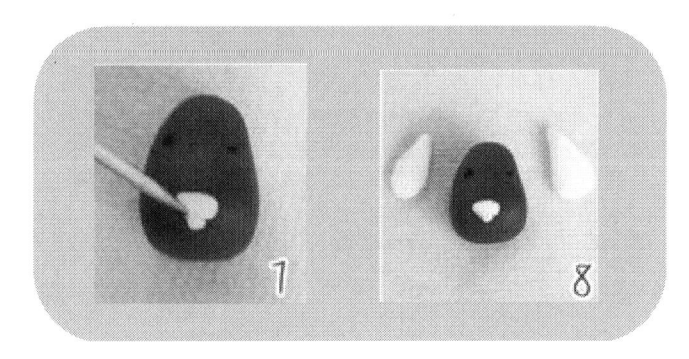

Sheep

- The sheep have fluffy white wool that helps keep them warm and a curved body shape. They have short legs and a short tail, and their face is covered by a thick coat of wool, except for the nose and eyes. They also have curved horns on their heads, but not all sheep have horns.

- Diet: Sheep are herbivores, meaning they only eat plants. They graze on grass, clover, and other green plants and shrubs. They need to eat a lot of food because their wool continues to grow and they also need to have a healthy diet to produce milk for their young.

- Reproduction: Female sheep are called ewes and male sheep are called rams. Ewes can have one to three lambs (ewes) at a time and usually give birth in the spring. Lambs are born with soft, fluffy wool and grow quickly, nursing from their mothers for several months.

- Behavior: Sheep are social animals and like to live in flocks. They follow a leading sheep, who is usually the strongest and most confident member of the flock. They are also very curious animals and love to explore their environment and play with their mates.

- Importance: Sheep have been domesticated by humans for thousands of years and play an important role in agriculture. They provide wool for clothing and textiles, and their meat is a staple food in many countries. In some areas, sheep are also used as work animals to help move other animals or equipment around the farm.

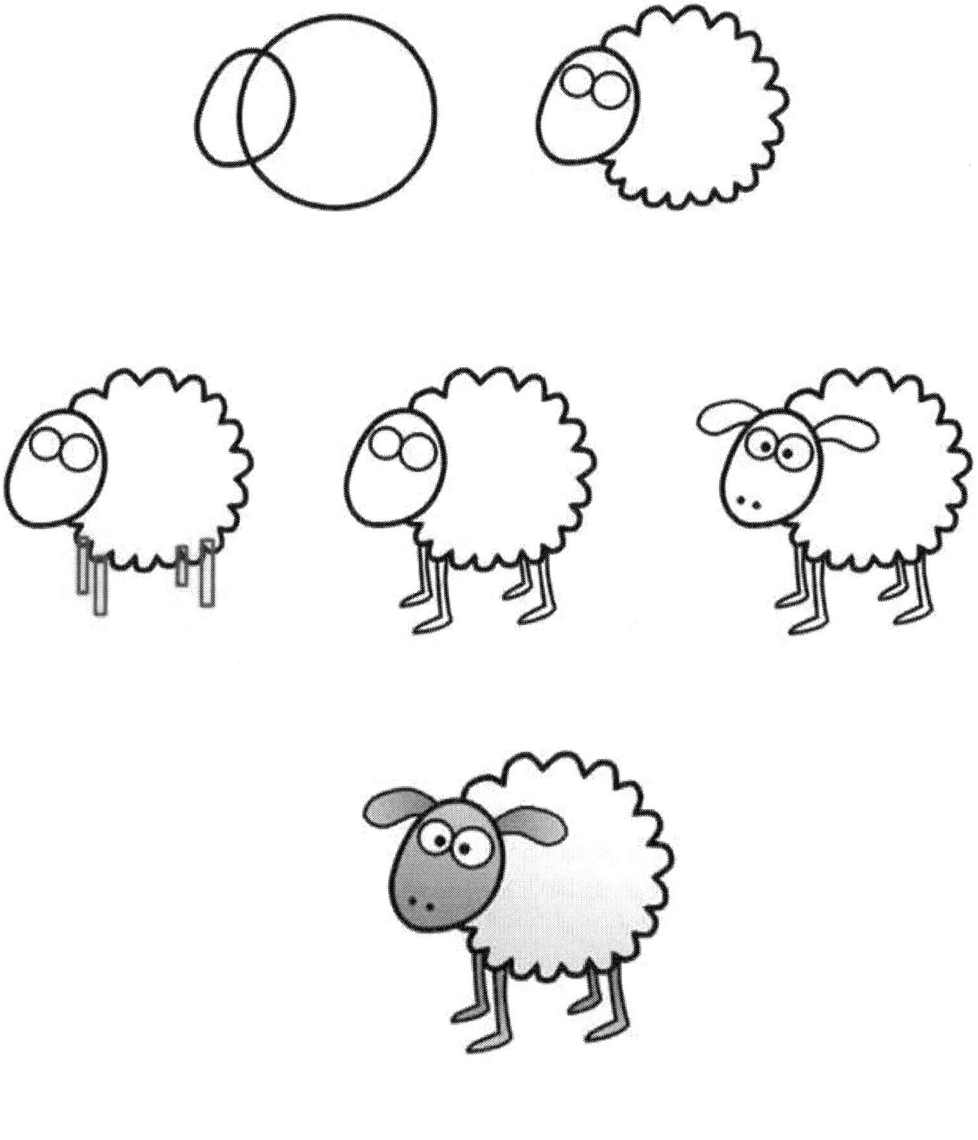

Draw here

Octopus

- **Octopuses are marine animals famous for their rounded bodies, bulging eyes, and eight long arms.**

- **They live in all the world's oceans but are particularly abundant in warm, tropical waters.**

- **Octopuses have a short life span. Some live less than 6 months, and larger species, such as the Pacific Giant Octopus, can live up to 5 years.**

- **Octopuses are very intelligent animals, probably the most intelligent invertebrates.**

- **Most octopuses expel a large blackish cloud of ink that helps them escape from predators.**

1. 2. 3.

4. 5. 6.

7. 8. 9.

Draw here

Clownfish

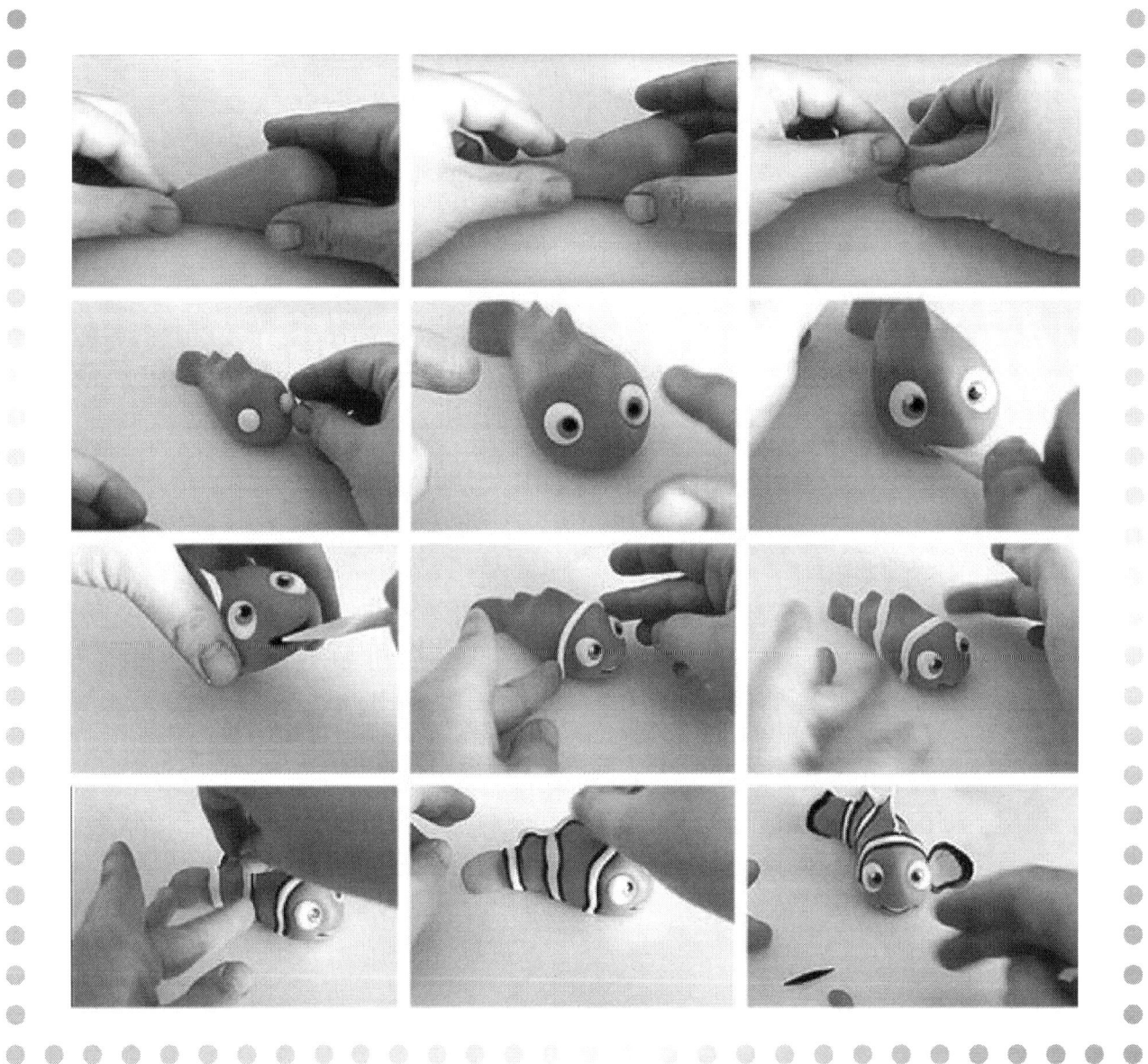

- Clownfish are nothing more than fish, which are also called anemone fish. Like all anemone fish, clownfish are related to sea anemones. It uses its host, both as shelter and to protect itself from predators, and, in return, the clownfish repel intruders and clean its host, removing parasites.

- Interesting facts about clownfish:
- 1. Most species of clownfish have an orange body with one or more white stripes. There are no obvious color differences between the male and the female, but the female is larger compared to the male. The clown fish can reach a length of up to 7-11 cm at maturity.

- 2. The clownfish is omnivorous, so it eats both meat and vegetables. In its natural environment, the clownfish obtains its food almost entirely by cooperating with its host, the anemone.

- 3. Clownfish mate throughout the year. After the female lays her eggs, the male comes to fertilize them.

- 4. Life expectancy
- The average life expectancy of fish is about 10 to 13 years.

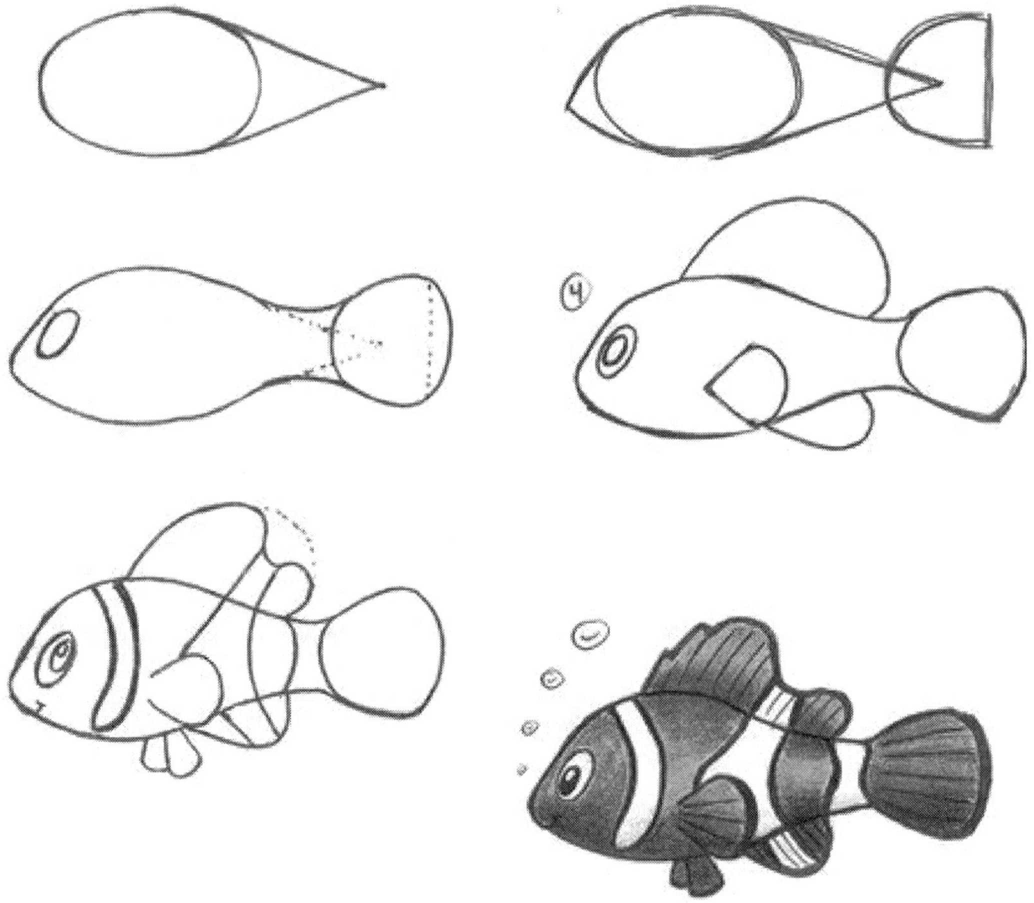
4

Draw here

Starfish

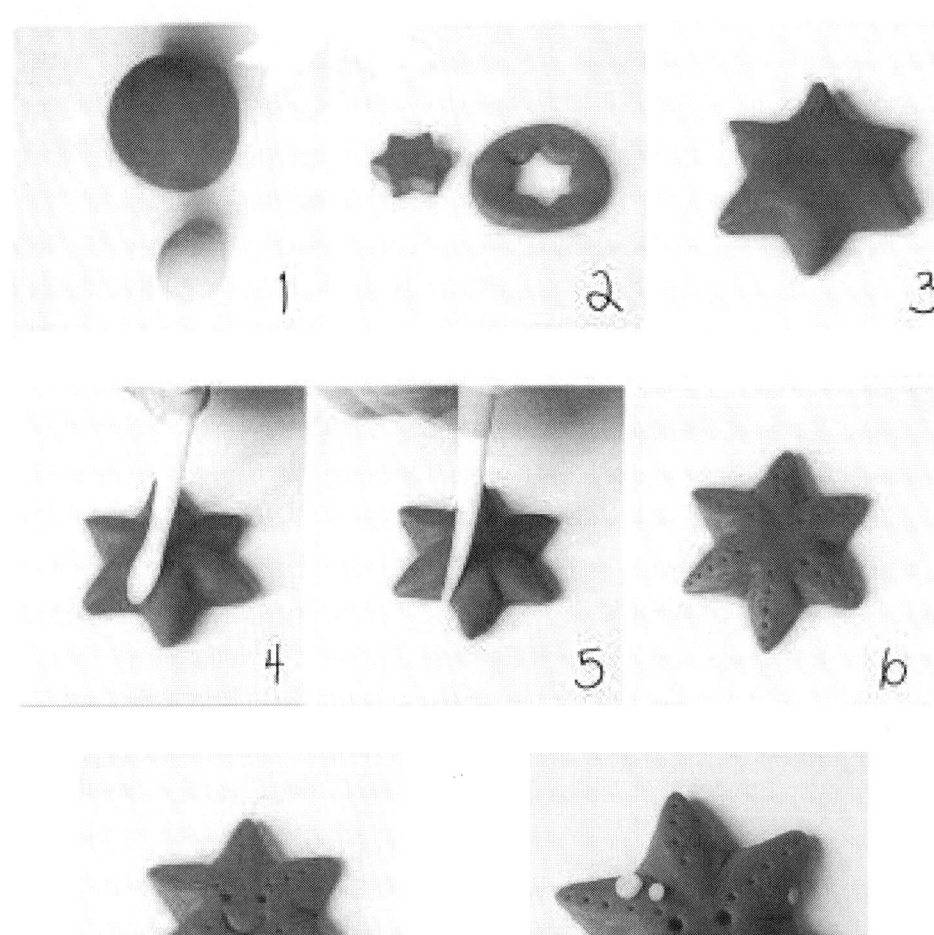

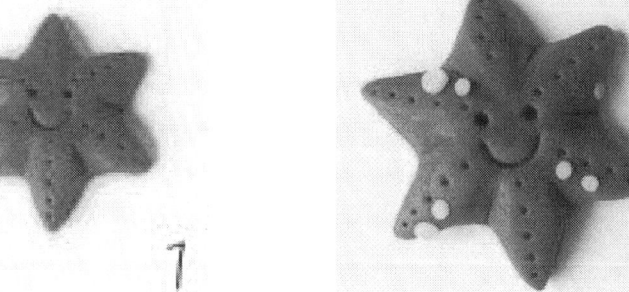

1 2 3
4 5 6
7

- Starfish are fascinating animals and we can find them in all the world's oceans.

- 1. Most have 5 arms, but there are species with 12, 24, or even 50 arms.

- 2. Like other sea creatures, starfish can regenerate their lost arms. Some species can even regenerate their entire body, starting from a single remaining arm. If attacked, some species can detach one of their arms to escape.

- 3. They have eyes at the end of each arm. However, I can't see very well, I can't see in detail, and I can only distinguish light and dark.

- 4. When we think of starfish, we imagine them as small animals that we can hold in the palm of our hand, but there are starfish that can even reach 1 meter.

- 5. According to National Geographic, there are approximately 2,000 species of starfish. They come in a wide variety of colors, sizes, number of arms, or with different textures.

- 6. They are carnivorous animals that feed, most often, on oysters, mollusks or snails.

- 7. They move using small tubular legs (small suction cups), which they have attached to their arms.

- 8. Some species live up to 5 years, while others can live up to 30 years.

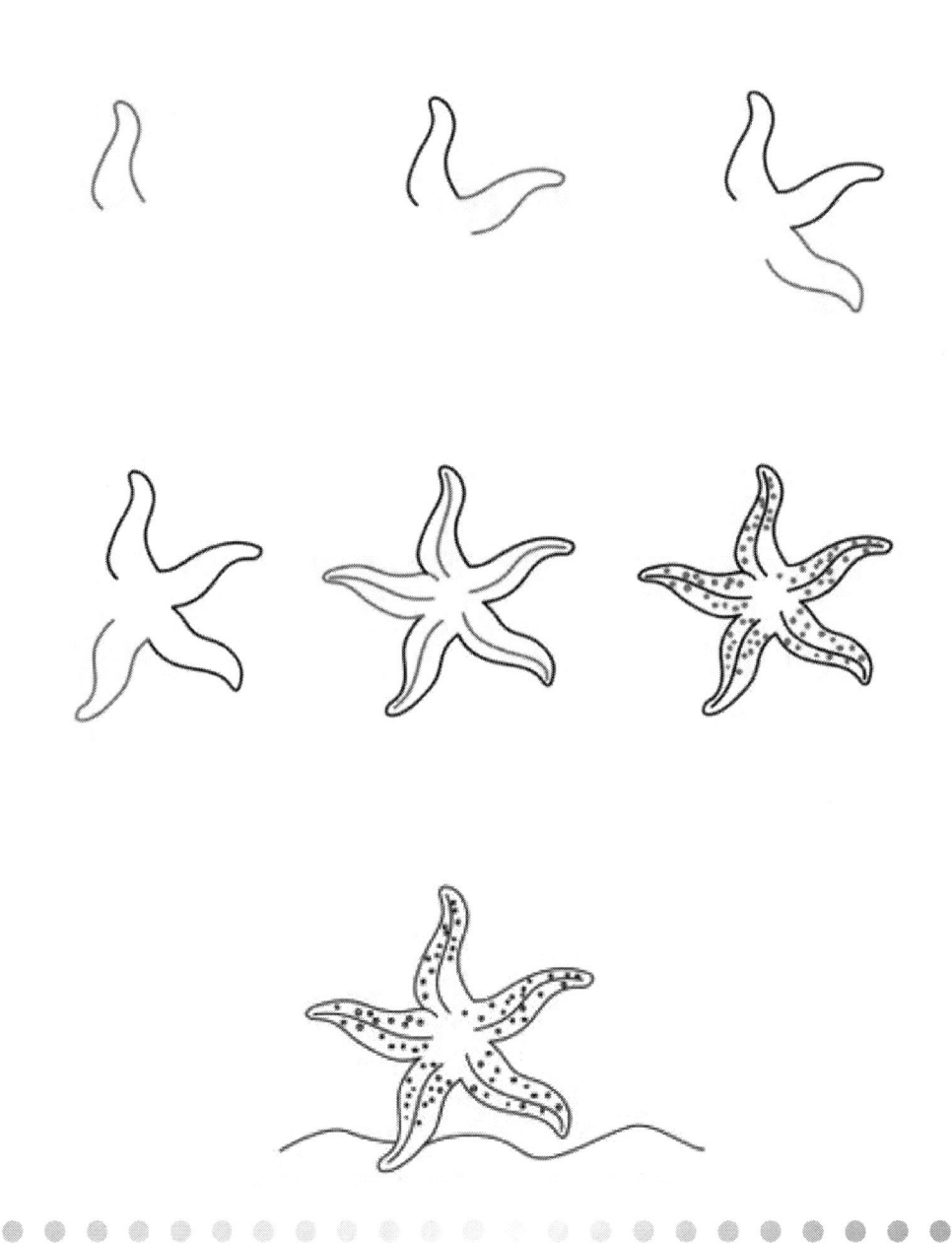

Draw here

Frog

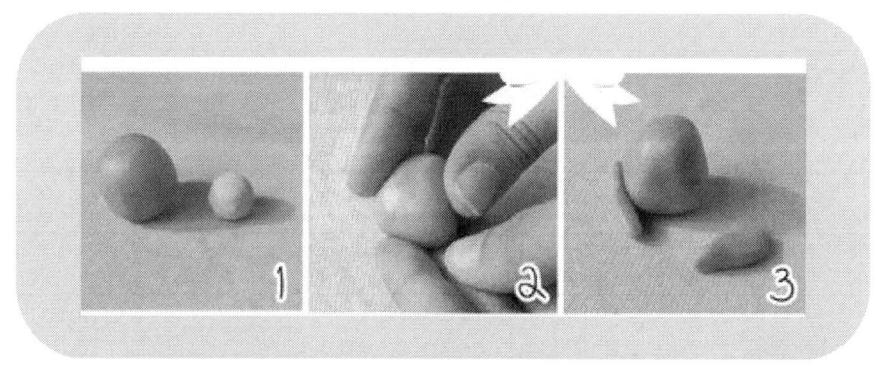

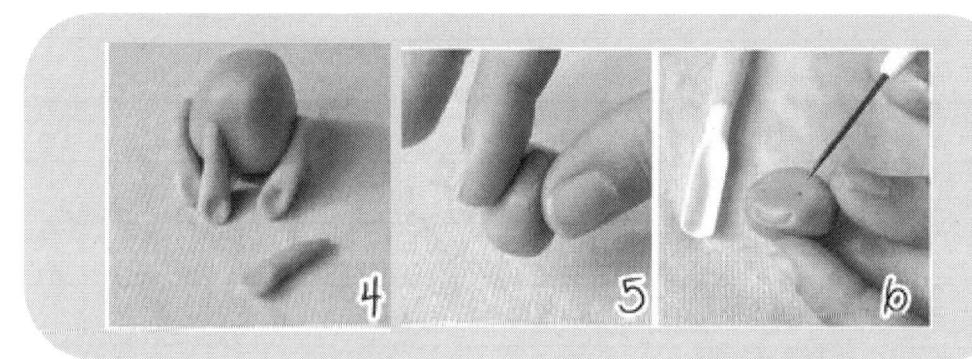

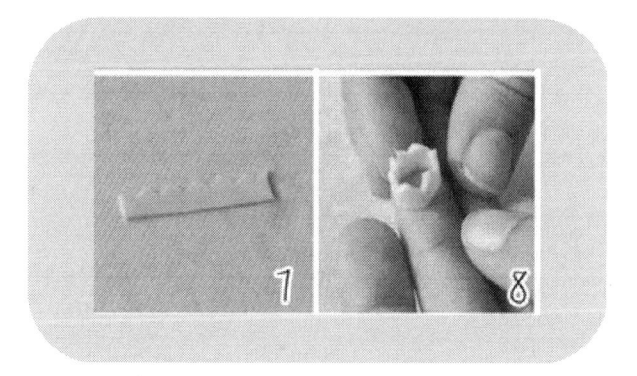

- A frog is a unique and interesting creature that lives near water sources such as ponds, lakes, or streams. It has slimy and moist skin which helps it stay cool in hot weather and it also protects it from predators. The frog's skin comes in different shades of green and sometimes brown, making it blend in perfectly with its surroundings.

- One of the most distinctive features of a frog is its big, bulgy eyes. These eyes are situated on the top of its head and help it see in the dark. They also can move independently, allowing the frog to have 360-degree vision. The frog's eyes are also connected to its long, sticky tongue which it uses to catch its food. With just a flick of its tongue, it can catch insects and other small prey.

- Frogs are great jumpers and they use their strong legs to leap into the air and land in the water. They can jump up to 20 times their body length in a single leap! This ability helps them escape predators and find food. Frogs are also great swimmers and they use their webbed feet to move quickly through the water.

- Another characteristic of a frog is its croaky voice. During the breeding season, male frogs sing to attract mates. They make a deep, croaky sound that can be heard from far away. The female frog then chooses the male with the most attractive croak to mate with.

- Frogs are important for the environment as they help keep insect populations in check.

1.

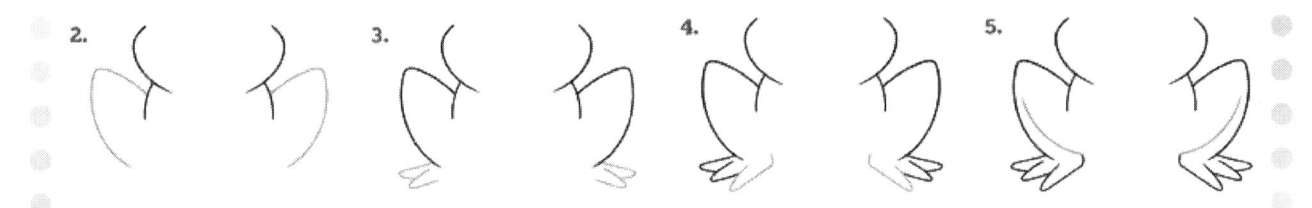

2. 3. 4. 5.

6. 7. 8. 9.

Draw here

Crocodile

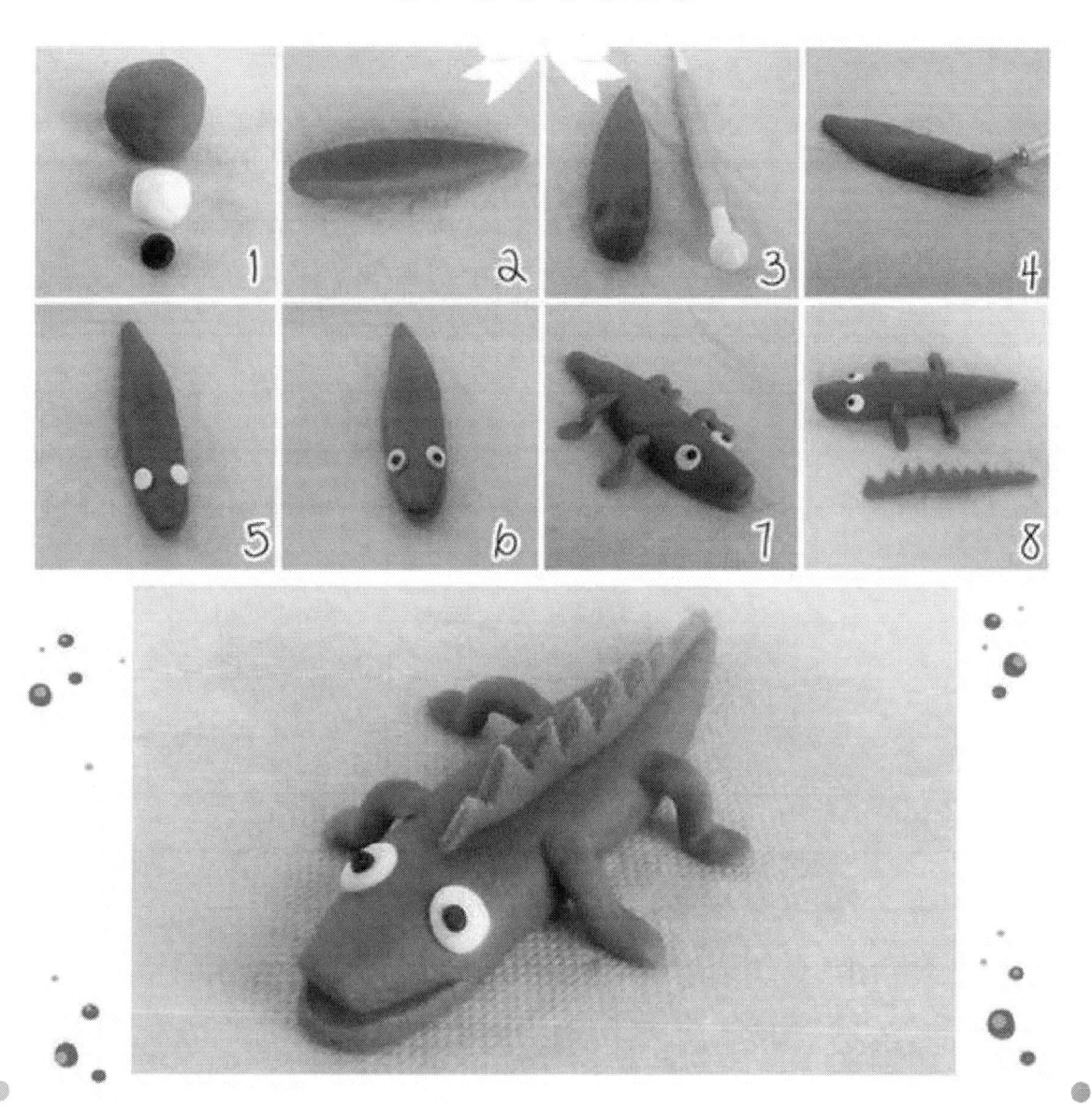

- A crocodile is a big and strong animal that lives in the water. They have a long bodies, big jaws, and sharp teeth. They are excellent swimmers and can hold their breath for a long time while they are hunting for food.
- Crocodiles have greenish-brown skin that helps them blend in with their surroundings and sneak up on their prey. They are also very fast and can dash on land, although they look awkward and slow.
- Crocodiles eat fish, birds, and other animals. They are also known to attack humans, so it's essential to be careful when you're near the water in areas where crocodiles live.
- Despite their fearsome reputation, crocodiles play an essential role in their ecosystem by controlling other animal populations and helping maintain a healthy balance in their environment.

1.
2.
3.
4.
5.
6.
7.
8.
9.

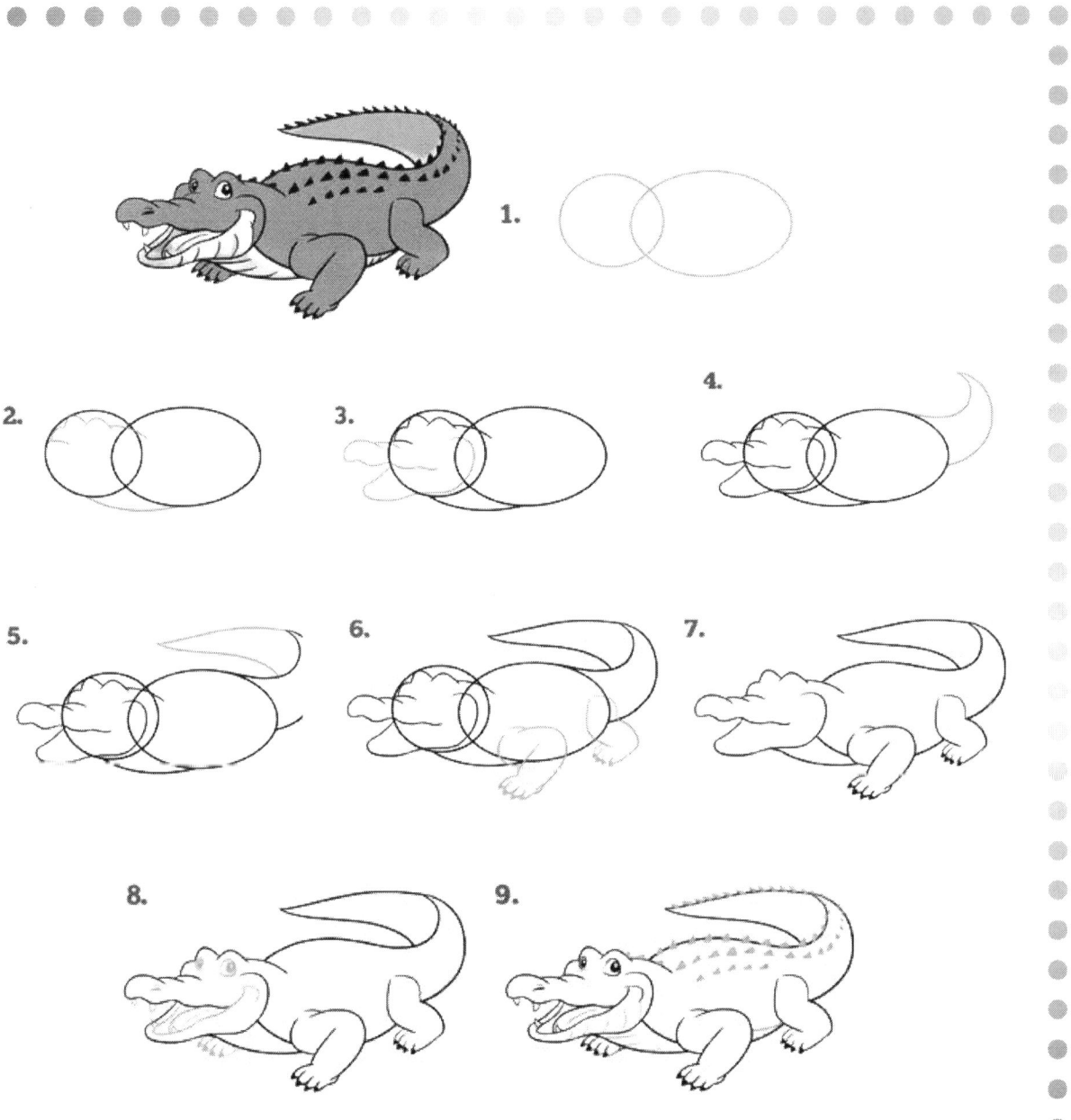

Draw here

Dragon-fly

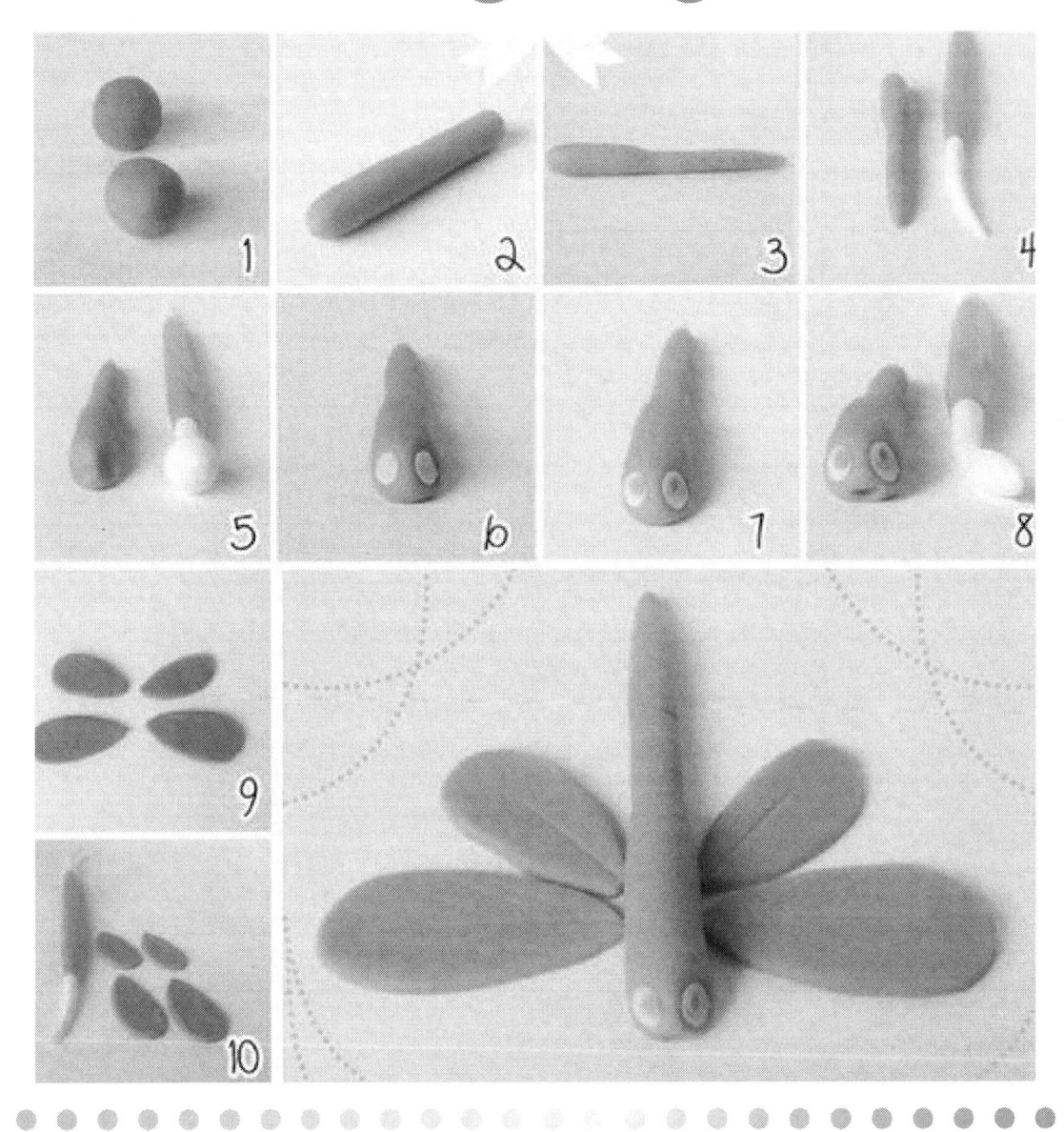

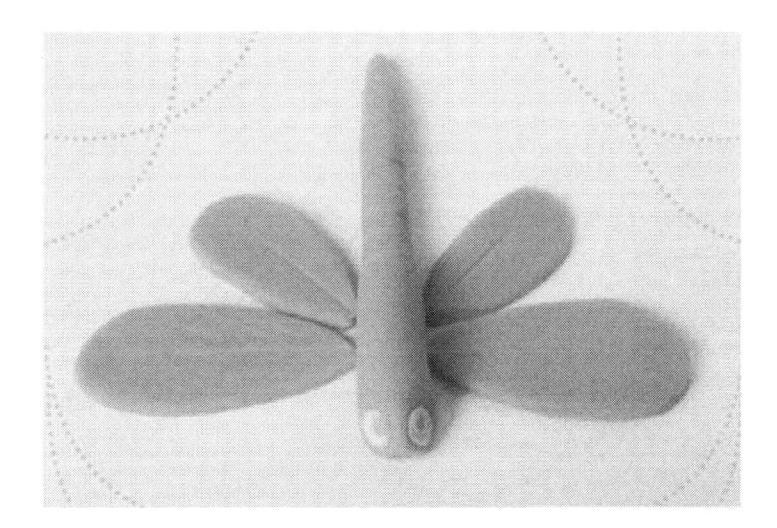

- Dragonflies have large compound eyes, which is their main sense organ. They have four transparent solid wings and long bodies.

- Dragonflies are usually found around lakes, ponds, streams, and wetlands.

- They are predators which eat mosquitoes and other small insects such as flies, bees, ants, and butterflies.

1.
2.
3.
4.
5.
6.
7.
8.
9.

Draw here

Ladybugs

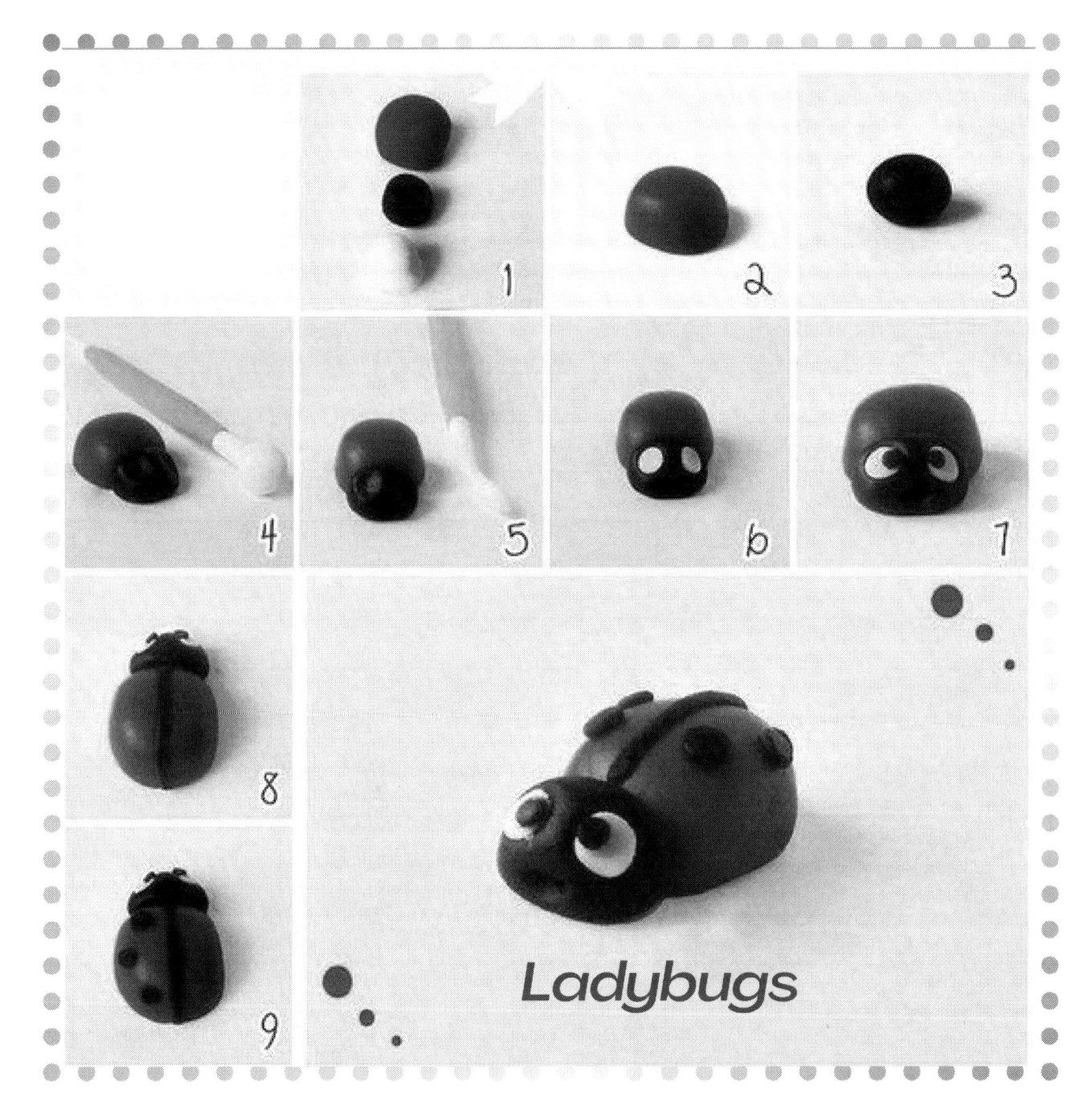

- Most people like ladybugs because they are pretty, graceful, and harmless to humans. But farmers love them because they eat aphids and other plant-eating pests.

- One ladybug can eat up to 5,000 insects in its lifetime! Most ladybugs have oval, dome-shaped bodies with six short legs.

- Depending on the species, they can have spots, stripes, or no markings at all. Seven-spotted ladybugs are red or orange with three spots on each side and one in the middle. They have a black heads with white patches on either side.

1. 2. 3.

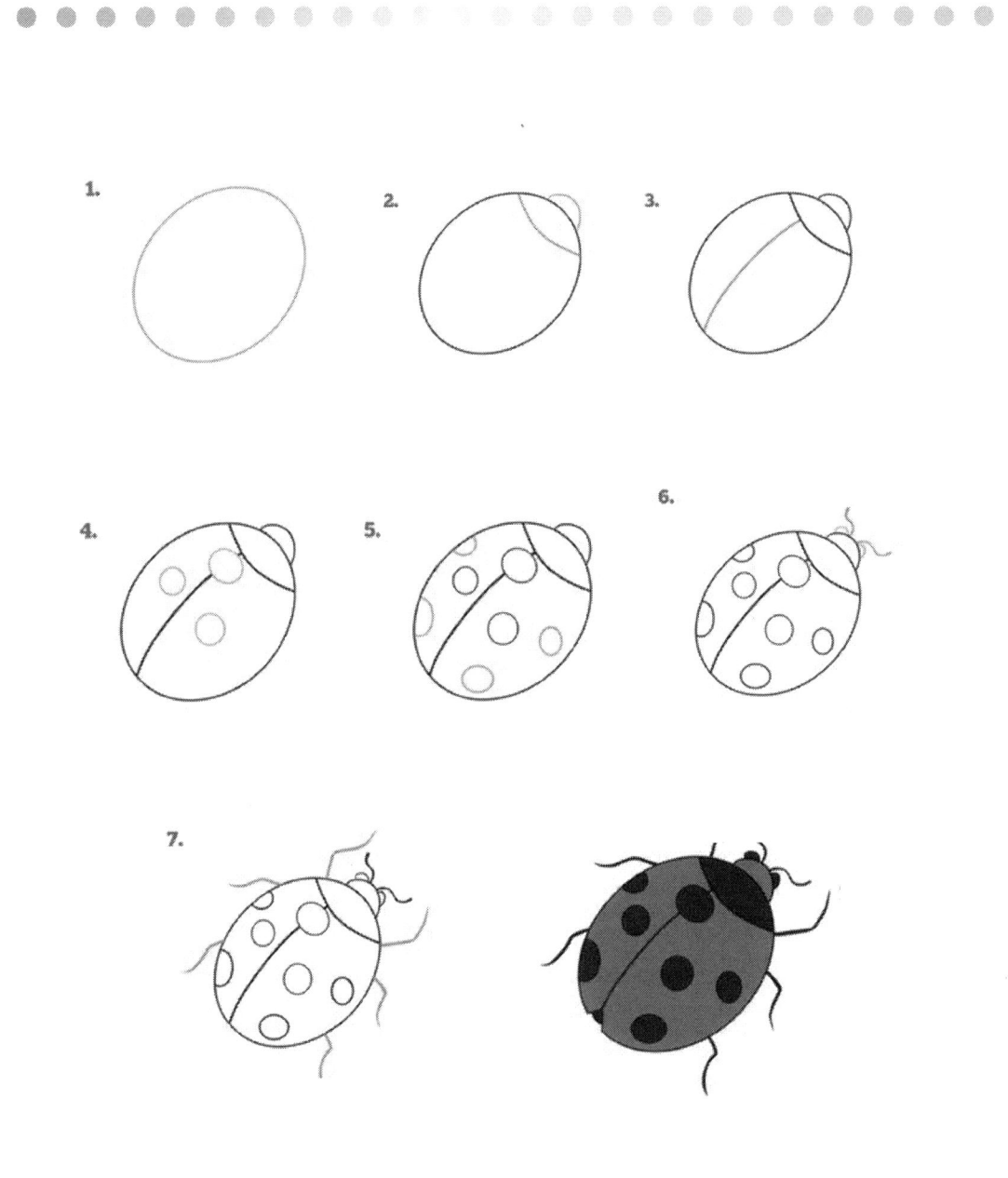

4. 5. 6.

7.

Draw here

© Copyright 2021 - All rights reserved.

You may not reproduce, duplicate or send the contents of this book without direct written permission from the author. You cannot hereby despite any circumstance blame the publisher or hold him or her to legal responsibility for any reparation, compensations, or monetary forfeiture owing to the information included herein, either directly or indirectly

Legal Notice: This book has copyright protection. You can use the book for personal purposes. You should not sell, use, alter, distribute, quote, take excerpts, or paraphrase in part or whole the material contained in this book without obtaining the permission of the author first.

Disclaimer Notice: You must take note that the information in this document is for casual reading and entertainment purposes only. We have made every attempt to provide accurate, up-to-date, and reliable information. We do not express or imply guarantees of any kind. The persons who read admit that the writer is not occupied in giving legal, financial, medical, or other advice. We put this book content by sourcing various places.

Please consult a licensed professional before you try any techniques shown in this book. By going through this document, the book lover comes to an agreement that under no situation is the author accountable for any forfeiture, direct or indirect, which they may incur because of the use of material contained in this document, including, but not limited to, — errors, omissions, or inaccuracies.

Hi!

My name is Bianca Colington. I sincerely hope you find my book to be helpful and fun.
Your kind reviews and comments will encourage me to make more books like this.
Write to me at b1anca.neve@yahoo.com

Thank you!
Bianca Colington

Manufactured by Amazon.ca
Bolton, ON